First published in 1981 by
Macmillan Children's Books
a division of Macmillan Publishers Limited
4 Little Essex Street, London WC2R 3LF
and Basingstoke
Associated companies throughout the world
Reprinted in 1982

Printed in Hong Kong

ISBN 0 333 30866 2

Editor: Miranda Ferguson
Designer: Julian Holland
Picture Researcher: Stella Martin
Photo Credits:
All-Sport; Archery International Publications;
Australian Information Service, London;
BBC Hulton Picture Library; British Library;
British Sports Association for the Disabled; David Charman;
Peter Clayton; Colorsport; Gerry Cranham;
Mary Evans Picture Library; Ken Gillham; Stephen Godfrey;
Golden Harvest Films; Sonia Halliday; Hamlyn Group;
G. David Hogg; Michael Holford; Lambeth Palace Library;
Mansell Collection; Leo Mason; Ian Murray;
Peter Newark's Western Americana; Popperfoto; Scala; Spectrum;
Sporting Pictures; Victoria and Albert Museum;
Werner Forman Archive; ZEFA

Kent, Graeme
    Fighting sports.
    1. Hand-to-hand fighting – Juvenile literature
    I. Title
    796.8   GV1111

    ISBN 0 333 30866 2

Fighting Sports

Graeme Kent

M

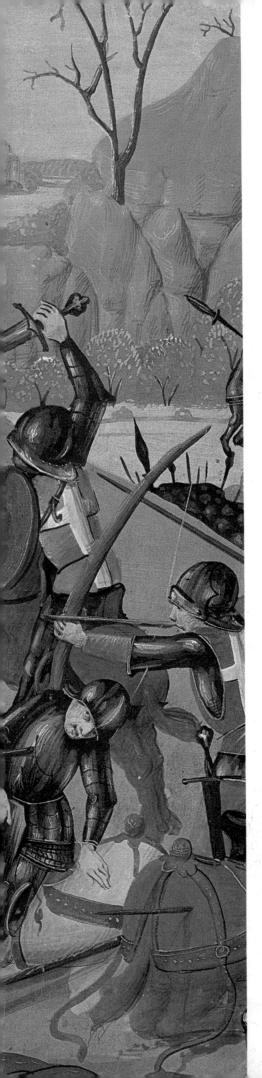

Contents

The Battle of Agincourt was fought on St Crispin's Day in 1415, between the English and the French. It was a conflict in which both traditional weapons of warfare and the newly discovered gunpowder were used to great effect.

Introduction

People have always fought with each other. The first men and women probably battled with sticks and stones over a piece of ground or the carcass of a dead animal.

As time passed men invented weapons of war. Flint axes and wooden spears gave way to metal swords and spears. Armies clashed on horseback or on foot. There were great battles in which thousands were killed. Some warriors developed great skill in the use of clubs, daggers and other weapons. The best fighters often became trainers, teaching the others the arts of war.

In this way, fighting skills were taken from the battlefield. They were used in the training of young people. Greek youths wrestled and boxed as part of their preparations for war. The Romans threw javelins. The Vikings used bows and arrows. Chiefs of tribes and leaders of nations encouraged their followers to take part in these fighting sports. They could thus be kept fit and ready for combat at short notice.

With the passing of time, conditions became more settled. Kings and emperors wanted to keep the peace. They decided that the energies of their young people could be diverted into sporting activities. So the various fighting sports that we know today gradually appeared. Such tests of skill and strength as boxing, wrestling, archery, shooting, the martial arts, swordsmanship and others, grew and changed until they became popular modern sports, many of them practised throughout the world.

In this book we shall look at these fighting sports. We shall see how they developed and the ways in which they are practised all over the world. Some of the great champions of these sports will be seen in action, as well as ordinary men and women, boys and girls.

The lull before the storm! Two gigantic Japanese Sumo wrestlers crouch down before one another, ready to explode into action. Using their great strength and weight they will try to knock one another out of the circle where they are wrestling.

The Sword

The Development of the Sword

The first men hunted wild animals with sharpened sticks and stone axes. Later, they discovered how to forge metal and made the sword, which was first used in battle about 3000 BC. The earliest sword known to man was found in the tomb of a king of Ur in the Middle East.

The early blades were made of bronze. It was not easy to keep their edges sharp. This meant that, at first, the weapons were only worn by the leaders of the fighters as a sign of their rank. These swords were sometimes used by gladiators in special contests of skill between individual swordsmen.

The use of the sword was popular throughout the world. One example of this is the so-called divine sword of Japan, used by a prince more than 2,000 years ago.

This hunting scene (above), dating back to the Bronze Age of pre-history, shows how men invented striking weapons with which to hunt wild animals.

Huge crowds gathered at the Colosseum in Rome to witness bouts between gladiators (below). Combats between individual swordsmen were very popular at the time.

Men soon realized that a great deal of skill was needed to wield a sword properly. Some Egyptian carvings made about 1000 BC show fighters being instructed at a special training school.

The ancient Greeks had many legends about their great warriors. In the *Iliad* the poet Homer tells how Paris, son of the king of Troy, fought a duel with Menelaus, king of Sparta. The goddess Venus favoured Paris and caused the sword of Menelaus to shatter on the prince's helmet. She then carried Paris safely away.

The Roman soldiers, who defeated the Greeks, were armed with short, stabbing swords which they used to great effect at close quarters.

The Greeks were skilled metalworkers, capable of designing both arms and armour. Their soldiers were among the first to wear body armour. They were equipped with bronze helmets, breast-plates and back-plates of bronze or iron, and metal leg-guards. They carried shields of leather and wood, and used a variety of weapons.

Greek legends are full of tales of epic contests between their heroes. One of their greatest warriors was Achilles, seen here on the left.

In the Middle Ages, the discovery of other forms of metal meant that stronger and sharper swords could be made by blacksmiths for noblemen. The first iron swords were very heavy and cumbersome. They were intended for defence as much as for attack. The weapons had edges on two sides and no hand-guards. They were wielded with both hands, rather like battle-axes.

Warriors of the time had no need of light and flexible swords. They wore heavy armour and helmets. They overcame their foes by battering away at their heads and bodies, hoping eventually to pierce their armour.

The invention of gunpowder in the 14th century brought about a great change in the nature of warfare. No longer was there such a need for heavily protected knights to charge at castle walls on their war-horses. To their dismay, the knights found that bullets were able to pierce their armour, so they discarded it. No longer did they need such heavy weapons. Instead they searched for lighter swords which were easier to wield.

The invention of steel (by mixing iron with carbon) resulted in the development of a much lighter sword. A Spanish captain called de Cordova invented the handguard. A new form of weapon was emerging.

There was now a need for instructors who could teach men how to use the new steel swords. Schools of fencing came into being.

Street brawls (above) were common in 14th-century Paris. A gentleman never knew when he might be attacked by footpads.

In the Middle East in medieval times, the possession of a steel sword was a sign of wealth and position. The blades were used on hunting expeditions (right).

When William of Normandy invaded England in 1066, he knew that he would have to rely on his swordsmen for the final battle. In the Battle of Hastings (below) the Normans lured the Saxons from their defensive positions and cut them down.

Beginnings of Fencing

Most men could handle the new light swords with ease, so the fencing masters began adapting swordsmanship so that it became an art in which anyone could take part.

The Spaniards developed a long, thin blade known as the rapier. This was adopted and perfected by the Italians, who were particularly skilful at fencing.

A French expert invented the fencing mask. This meant that if the swordsmen were also well padded they could take part in bouts without risking serious injury. Soon fencing became a popular sport among the rich.

The art varied from country to country. Some of the first fencing schools were in Germany, and here the rapier soon replaced the thick iron blade. The French used short swords. The Italian fencing schools tried to mix the better practices of all the different forms.

The fencing schools drew up rules and codes of conduct for swordsmen. They tried out different types of blade – some with points, others with cutting edges. Fencing masters toured Europe, setting up schools in most cities and spreading the art of swordsmanship. Exhibition matches were held before large audiences.

A good 19th-century fencing school or gymnasium provided its students with proper masks and body-padding (above). The sport was particularly popular with German university students who tried to discard the mask because a duelling scar on the cheek was considered a mark of distinction.

Among the different types of fencing practised in the 17th century was the French fashion of using both a sword and dagger at the same time (left).

The early Italian fencing masters developed the art of fencing (right).

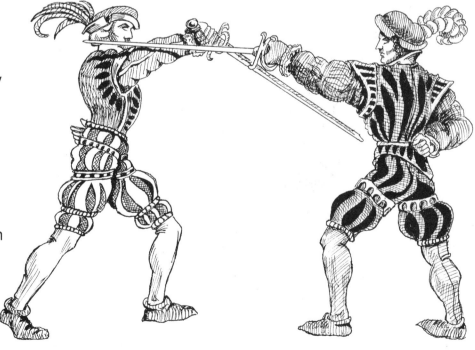

Duelling

In most European countries, it became the custom to wear a sword and to receive some instruction in its use. When the rapier was replaced by the small-sword, which could be worn anywhere, the habit became even more widespread. In the 17th and 18th centuries this led to the growth of duelling. If men did not agree over something, or if someone thought that he had been insulted, the result was often a challenge to a fencing bout with no form of protection. Some duels ended when one of the participants had drawn blood from his opponent, but many were continued until one of the duellists had killed the other.

Soon there were as many rules and ceremonies attached to duelling as there had been to organized fencing bouts in the schools.

Most countries banned duelling. There were heavy penalties imposed for those found taking part in a contest of this sort, but it was a very long time before the practice died away.

The Duke of Buckingham, son of King Charles I's favourite courtier, was as adept with the sword as any man of his time. In 1668, he fought a duel (right) with another nobleman who accused Buckingham of trifling with his wife's affections. Buckingham slew his opponent.

In 1787, there took place in London a fencing bout between two most unusual people (below). The match was an exhibition bout before the Prince of Wales. The two contestants were M. De St George, one of the best-known fencing masters of his time (seen on the left), and the incredible Chevalier d'Eon Beaumont. D'Eon sometimes dressed as a woman in order to obtain information to pass on to the French. After his death his body was dug up and examined to make sure he had been a man!

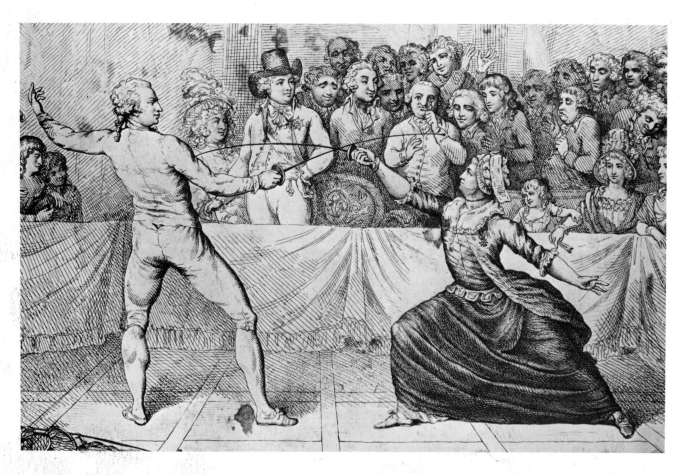

Duels usually took place early in the morning when there were few people about and less chance of being disturbed. Each man had his second and there was usually a doctor in attendance. If the authorities heard of a duel they would forbid it to take place. One of the last contests between men of note took place in 1897, between Prince Henri d'Orleans and the Comte de Turin (below).

Olympics, Positions and Foils

Today, both men and women take part in the sport of fencing, and there are fencing clubs in most countries. The three basic swords are the foil and the épée, which have points, and the sabre, which has both a point and a cutting edge. The object of the sport is to touch an opponent with the sword and to avoid being hit in return.

In addition to the swords, the basic equipment needed consists of a face mask, a padded jacket and gloves. The point of a blade is always covered with a 'button' to avoid injury to the contestants.

In competitive fencing, foils and épées are fitted with electronically operated spring-loaded points. When a 'hit' is scored on an opponent it is registered on a piece of apparatus which is connected to the blade. There are both individual and team events in fencing. There are usually three or four members in each team. A jury of experts is in charge.

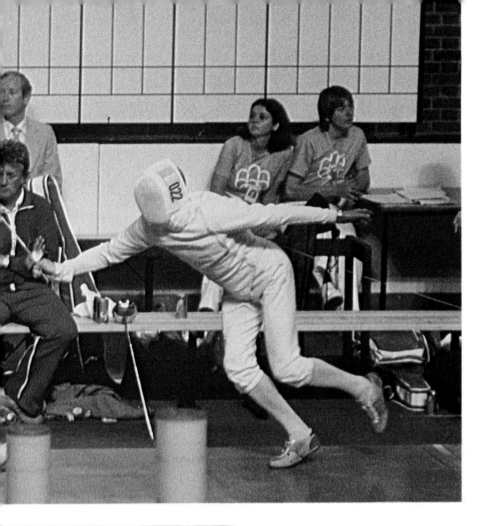

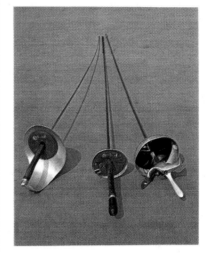

The basic swords used in fencing are the thin, flexible foil; the heavier and more rigid épée; and the sabre which has cutting edges along the front of the blade and part of the back.

Fencing is a sport in which both men and women take part in the Olympic Games (above). There are individual and team events. A great fencing scandal occurred in the pentathlon competition in the 1976 Olympics in Montreal. In this illustration the Russian fencer, Boris Onishenko, is seen stepping back after registering a 'hit' on his opponent. In fact no hit had taken place. After an investigation, the Russian was accused of rigging his sword-point, and was disqualified from the competition.

The first women famed for handling swords were two female pirates, Anne Bonny and Mary Read. Today, many women enjoy the sport of fencing, like the two seen (left) taking part in the team competition at the Montreal Olympics.

A fencer in a mask and padded jacket is adopting an *en garde* ('on guard') position. The fencer stands up straight, with his feet at right angles and his right shoulder and toe pointing at his opponent.

15

Swordplay

The increasing use of swords from early times meant that there was always work for the sword-makers. The Saxons, whose swords were simple, straight weapons with hilts of horn, told in their legends of the magical blades made by the smith Weland.

In the following centuries, the smiths were always ready to experiment with their craft and to design new swords. The Vikings and the Normans had straight blades that could be used for cutting and stabbing. By the 14th century, the designers were producing 'falchions', single-edged weapons with a wide, curving blade not unlike the flashing scimitars of the Turks that the Crusaders would have seen.

The fencing masters of the different nations were often very jealous of one another. In the 16th century an Englishman, George Silver, scoffed at and challenged experts from other countries to meet him in combat, but they all refused his challenge.

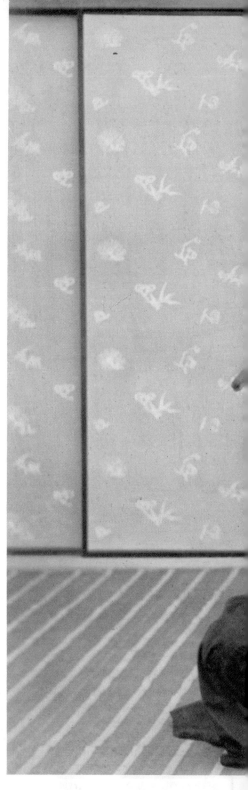

Fencing schools and displays of swordsmanship flourished in Japan and its provinces from an early age. This illustration (left) shows two women engaged in a fencing exhibition in North Korea in about 1800. The champions of the sport in Japan were said to be able to cut in half arrows fired at them from only a short distance.

The great Japanese sword-makers of the Middle Ages made their blades by melting down iron in furnaces, hammering out the shape of the blade and then working charcoal into it before sharpening and polishing the edge.

The best-known form of swordsmanship in Japan today is kendo. For this mode of fighting the participants wear ornate armour and padding. The 'shinai', or sword, is made of wood and is about 118 centimetres long.

Uttering shrill cries, the kendo athlete tries to strike his opponent on certain stated parts of his body. A bout lasts only three minutes and the players are encased in helmet, gloves, breast-plate and stomach-guard. The 'shinai' or sword is made of four strips of bamboo bound together. A referee awards points.

Different forms of sword-fighting are in use all over the world. Two warriors in Thailand (left) are shown practising their art.

Expert swordsmen are sometimes needed to arrange duels and fights for the stage and screen. The stunt men here (below) are preparing for a battle scene in the film *The Charge of the Light Brigade*, which is set in the Crimea during the 19th century. Today, most actors receive instruction in the art of fencing during their training.

The sword is still recognized as a symbol of wealth and power. Modern collectors pay large sums for well-designed blades. Recently, over £20,000 changed hands for a beautiful jewelled rapier designed in the 17th century by Israel Schuech.

Armies continue to use the sword on parades and for some ceremonial occasions. Swords are often presented to young officers who have done well in their training. In England, the monarch confers a knighthood on a chosen subject by tapping him on each shoulder with the flat of the sword-blade.

The Scots include sword-dancing in many of their traditional celebrations and Highland Games. A dancer skips lightly between two blades which are crossed on the ground at his feet.

An unusual and very dangerous modern use of the sword is that of sword-swallowing. Some circus performers have swallowed blades which are over half a metre in length.

Actors and producers often call in a stunt arranger to organize a stage or screen duel. His job is to make a fight historically accurate, exciting to watch and reasonably safe for the actors taking part! Sir Henry Irving, the great actor-manager of the 19th century, used to fix flints to the blades of the swords used in his stage duels so that they would give off sparks when struck. Later he tried to have the blades electrically wired so that they would produce even more spectacular flashes, but his actors did not like receiving electric shocks!

Today the sword is often used in ceremonial dances which represent the grim sword battles of earlier days. An example of this is the Turkish Bursa sword-dancing seen here. Sword-dancing was also favoured by Nordic nations when celebrating great battles and the custom remains to this day.

Wrestling
Early Wrestling

Primitive men may have grappled with each other round the camp fire to see who was the strongest and best able to stand up to the wild beasts which lay in wait everywhere. From these early wrestling bouts developed the holds and throws used in wrestling today – the headlock, the takedown, the flying mare, and many others.

By the time of the first great civilization of Egypt, more than 5,000 years ago, wrestling was a highly skilled art. The Egyptians trained their soldiers to wrestle, as well as in the use of the javelin and bows and arrows.

All the ancient heroes were expected to be good wrestlers. There is a legend from Babylonia which is more than 4,000 years old and tells how the giant king Gilgamesh offended the gods. In order to punish him, the gods created a wild man. Gilgamesh and the wild man met in a fierce wrestling match which raged all over the market-place. Despite the fight, Gilgamesh and the wild man became great friends. Legends like this made wrestling very popular.

Wall-paintings found at Beni Hasan in Egypt (above) are almost 4,000 years old. They show wrestlers in training.

When Gilgamesh (below), the renowned Babylonian wrestler, met the wild man in a wrestling contest, the fight raged all over the village.

In ancient China, as in Egypt, wrestling was as much a part of army training as fist-fighting and spear-throwing.

It was in the island civilization of Crete 3,000 years ago that a form of wrestling first became a popular spectator sport, and not just a preparation for warfare. This was the famous bull-dancing. A team of three, two girls and a boy, would be pitted against an enraged bull in the arena, as an entertainment for an excited crowd.

The bull-dancers were usually specially trained slaves and their lives were often short. When the angry bull charged at them, one girl would grasp the horns of the beast. The youth would vault over her, turning a somersault on the bull's back. Then he would leap off into the arms of the second girl. If any member of the team made a mistake in the arena, all three were in danger of being gored to death by the enraged bull.

Wrestling was also a popular sport with the ancient Jews, and a champion wrestler was a man of great importance. In the Old Testament of the Bible, there is a story about Jacob wrestling all night with a stranger. In the end, Jacob lost the contest and the stranger turned out to be an angel. Jacob hurt his leg during the bout but afterwards received the angel's blessing.

Some Chinese wrestlers (above) performed before the emperor, but most of them did it as part of their military training.

The Minoan bull-dancers were slaves trained from an early age. The youth in each team wore a yellow loin-cloth, while the girls wore yellow girdles.

The Development of Wrestling

The greatest Greek wrestler was Milo, the winner of six Olympic titles. In order to develop his strength he was reputed to have lifted a calf onto his shoulders every day until it was fully grown, and to have carried a young bull round the Olympic stadium before killing it with one blow from his fist.

Wrestling was also practised before enthusiastic crowds in the Roman arena. Commodus, who became emperor in AD 180, claimed to have won more than 700 bouts. It is doubtful, however, if the professional wrestlers would try very hard when fighting against their master.

In Greek wrestling, a contest ended when one wrestler forced any part of the trunk of his opponent to touch the ground.

One of these two Roman wrestlers (right) has forced his opponent to the ground in an arm-lock. Wrestling was a popular sport in the Roman arena, but spectators found the Greek style too static, so changes were made in the rules.

Commodus met his end when his enemies hired a wrestler to drug and then strangle him.

Wrestling became even more popular during the 4th and 5th centuries when professional wrestlers began wandering from country to country, performing at fairs and markets. Princes also took an interest in the sport. In India it became the custom for each moghul to have his own champion and for these wrestlers to grapple for an engraved club and the championship of all India.

In Japan in AD 858, two sons of the emperor Buntoku wrestled to see who would succeed their father. Seven centuries later, Francis I of France challenged Henry VIII of England to a bout after a team of English wrestlers had beaten the French. The royal wrestlers were stopped by their courtiers.

Wrestlers took part in tournaments in Persia thousands of years ago (below). Persian wrestling was much faster than the Greek style and competitors had to be very strong in order to manage the heavy lifting involved.

Two wrestlers in India (above) are about to start a contest. There was a great deal of ceremony attached to these contests and India was one country where women wrestlers also took part in tournaments.

Wrestling Exponents

Wrestling had been popular in North and South America long before the first Europeans landed. It became a favourite sport among the early settlers.

Before he became president of the United States, Abraham Lincoln once engaged in a wrestling match while he was working in a store in New Salem. He threw Jack Clayton, a local gang-leader. Clayton's gang wanted to attack the victor, but Clayton called them off, saying that he had been beaten fairly.

The first generally acknowledged champion of the world was William Muldoon, who claimed the title in 1880. He was a former soldier and New York policeman who had fought in the American Civil War.

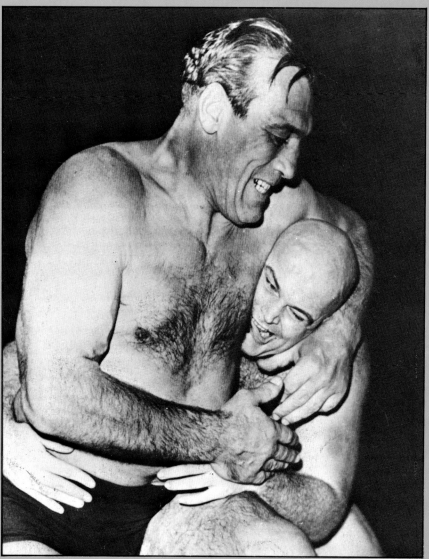

Georges Hackenschmidt, the 'Russian Lion', was the best-known European wrestler at the beginning of the 20th century. An enormously strong man, Hackenschmidt was such a good wrestler that he won most of his bouts in the first round. His English manager persuaded him to try and make his wrestling look more difficult. Accordingly, Hackenschmidt began to allow his opponents to last a few rounds before he pinned them to the canvas.

In 1904, Hackenschmidt defeated Madrali, the 'Terrible Turk', at Olympia in London. So many people wanted to see the contest that London had its first great traffic-jam.

The most successful boxer-turned-wrestler was the Italian Primo Carnera, seen here (left) holding an opponent in a headlock. Carnera was cheated out of most of his ring earnings as a boxer and was forced to take up wrestling in order to earn a living.

Wrestlers are in great demand for films, where they often play the part of villains. The Japanese grappler (above), wrestling under the name of Tosh Togo, achieved fame in the James Bond film *Goldfinger,* in which he played the evil Oddjob.

Billy Two Rivers (left), a genuine Red Indian, used many tribal practices in his wrestling. If an opponent goaded him beyond endurance, he would perform an Indian war-dance round the ring, utter a war-whoop and then launch himself upon his luckless adversary with a series of 'tomahawk-chops' to the throat with the side of his hand.

In Great Britain, one of the largest and most popular super-heavyweights is the well-named Big Daddy, seen (above) fighting the bald 'Kojak' Kirk. Big Daddy has had a series of ring-shattering bouts with the even bigger Giant Haystacks. Most of the super-heavyweights make a speciality of the fall known as the 'Big Splash', which consists of falling on an inert opponent.

Professional wrestlers throughout the ages have adopted many different styles of grappling. The first wrestlers who toured the fairs in the Middle Ages would take on the local champion using the style favoured in that region.

As time passed the professionals tried to find one style that they could use anywhere. For a time, the 'collar-and-elbow' method was popular. Wearing strong jackets, each wrestler grasped the other by the collar and the elbow. This hold could not be released until one man had been thrown to the ground.

In Europe, many wrestlers used the Russian 'belt' style. Both wrestlers wore stout belts and tried to swing each other off balance by grabbing the belts.

Towards the end of the 19th century, this gave way to the Greco-Roman style of wrestling. In this no tripping was allowed and all the holds had to be above the waist. A contest ended when a wrestler had both shoulders pressed to the mat. Some champions became so skilled at this form of wrestling that it was almost impossible to throw them. One of William Muldoon's matches lasted for more than nine hours.

The crowds found this form of wrestling boring, so Greco-Roman wrestling was replaced by the 'catch-as-catch-can' style, which allowed a greater variety of throws and stipulated that holds could only be applied for a certain time. Later, catch-as-catch-can was replaced in the United States by the even wilder 'all-in' style, and in Europe by free-style wrestling, in which a round lasted for only five minutes.

Amateur wrestling bouts, like the match between children (left) and the Olympic match (right), are now restricted to short periods of time. This is because a Russian and a Swede grappled for more than 10 hours in a bout in the 1912 Olympics in Stockholm. A great furore was caused at the 1952 Olympics in Helsinki when the Turkish wrestlers arrived too late and were banned.

In the 1930s, promoters tried all sorts of gimmicks to draw the crowds to wrestling matches. In Germany, bouts between women wrestling in a sea of mud were popular, and the idea was introduced into England. This bout (left) took place in Clapham in 1938.

The Cumberland and Westmoreland style of wrestling involves the two competitors holding one another with their arms round each other's bodies (right). A man loses the bout if he releases his grip or if he is thrown to the ground.

A bout between two Baiote women wrestlers in Africa (below). The champion on the left wears a garter to symbolize her superiority in the sport.

Modern Variations

For centuries different styles of amateur wrestling have been practised by young men and sometimes by women, just for the love of the sport.

In Turkey, wrestling continues to attract huge audiences. Dozens of young men, their bodies covered in oil and their breeches soaked in water, grapple in pairs until there are just two men left to contest the final. The bouts are fought out to the accompaniment of music from flutes and drums, and a tournament can last for three days.

In Africa, the Latuko tribe counts wrestling as one of its main sports and still has its champions. Thousands of miles away in Mongolia, wrestlers can trace the history of their sport back to the time of the mighty conqueror Ghengis Khan. In Mongolia, as in India, there are no weight divisions, so the heaviest wrestlers usually win.

Wrestling has long been a sport at the Highland Games celebrations in Scotland (right). A contest between Scottish and English wrestlers took place in the reign of Henry VIII. Now rules drawn up by a Scot called Donald Dinnie are used.

The best of all the amateur wrestlers can meet every four years at the Olympic Games in two styles, Greco-Roman and free-style.

In 1896, when the first of the modern Olympiads was held, wrestling was one of the sports included. By 1920, both the Greco-Roman and the catch-as-catch-can championships were being contested at different weights. The catch-as-catch-can method became known as free-style.

Bouts were limited to fifteen minutes for the catch-as-catch-can and twenty minutes for the Greco-Roman. No holds below the waist were allowed in the latter style. Bouts in both styles ended when an opponent's shoulder-blades were pinned to the canvas. If neither wrestler could pin the other then a bout was decided on points.

In the Olympic wrestling bouts competitors have marks deducted for various errors. This system was adopted to encourage all wrestlers to grapple as hard as possible.

Sumo Wrestling

The gigantic Sumo wrestlers of Japan are as famous as pop stars. Although they are enormously fat, they are very light on their feet. The wrestlers train for years to produce this combination of bulk and speed.

The first recorded wrestling match in Japan took place in 23 BC. It was won by a grappler called Sukune. Sukune is now the patron of all Japanese wrestlers.

Sumo wrestling became well-established by the 17th century. Special schools were set up for the training of young men. Sumo wrestlers married the daughters of other grapplers in the hope that their sons would be big enough to follow in their footsteps.

Successful wrestlers were placed in one of three grades and allowed to wear an embroidered apron as a sign of their status.

Sumo champions line up before a competition in their ceremonial kimonos (below). Beneath the gowns the champions wear equally ornate loin-cloths. A champion will clap his hands to secure the attention of the gods before he begins to wrestle. Most Sumo bouts last only a few minutes. Everything depends on timing. If a heavy wrestler can time his shoulder-charge to perfection, few men can withstand it.

Great crowds gather to watch Sumo tournaments today. Bouts take place in a circular ring which is four metres in diameter. At the beginning of each contest there is a long ceremony.

The contest begins with two wrestlers facing each other with both hands on the ground. They circle slowly, waiting for an opportunity to attack. When one man sees his chance he advances and clutches his opponent. The two men rock backwards and forwards around the ring, heaving mightily. The bout ends when one wrestler has been pushed out of the ring or thrown off his feet.

Despite their bulk, Sumo wrestlers are very supple. They train their muscles by getting friends to twist their limbs into all sorts of positions, and then they sit in this contorted fashion for hours.

A Sumo competitor being thrown. In the early days of the sport a fallen wrestler was then trampled to death! A young Sumo wrestler is recruited soon after his 11th birthday and spends up to four hours a day preparing for the sport.

Holds and Throws

It's never too early to begin! Schoolboy wrestlers can often be seen in action. Both competitors are on the canvas and the fighter behind is in an attacking position. Next, he will try to turn his opponent. The wrestler in front will do his best to block his opponent's efforts.

Still on the ground one young wrestler has secured a half-nelson hold with step through. A half-nelson is one in which an arm is put under an opponent's arms and pressed against the back of his neck. This can render the opponent helpless and immobile.

Ground wrestling is a complex art. In this picture one wrestler is beginning an arm roll which would throw his opponent over his shoulder. In ground wrestling, speed and anticipation are almost as important to the competitor as skill, as everything depends on outmanoeuvring an opponent.

Strength is a great advantage to a wrestler. In this illustration, one wrestler is trying to force the other down onto the canvas, so that he may turn him and perhaps secure a fall. A useful skill is to use surprise tactics and catch the adversary off his guard.

There are a number of different lifts used in wrestling. All of them require strength and timing if they are to be successful. This one is a standing fireman's lift. From this position it should be possible to take or throw an opponent to the ground.

A pinfall! All wrestlers do their best to build up a points lead by securing the best holds and throws, but most of them prefer to pin an adversary's shoulders to the canvas and end the bout that way, like this boy has in the picture. It is one of the more dramatic ways of ending a bout.

The complex cradle move has almost been completed and one wrestler is nearly in a position to pin opponent's shoulders to the canvas. The wrestler underneath will try to spin out or secure his release in some other way if he can possibly manage it.

The end of a tournament is a happy event for the victors, but not so happy for the losers. A schoolboy champion has received a gold medal in his weight class, and is standing triumphantly on the rostrum with the silver and bronze medal winners.

Tug-of-War

Tug-of-war is one of the few sports in which a team has to go backwards in order to win! Like most other fighting sports, its history can be traced back over thousands of years. The ancient Greeks trained their soldiers to drag heavy weapons and wagons containing supplies over difficult ground by making them pull on ropes. In order to make this training more interesting the soldiers were divided into teams and pulled against each other.

From this developed the sport that was to become popular for centuries at fairs and markets all over the world. It was taken up by the military again in the 18th and 19th centuries when heavy artillery pieces had to be hauled up the sides of hills. In order to keep their troops in condition, the tug-of-war was introduced by officers at most soldiers' sports meetings. In the navy, pulling on 'sheets' (ropes) to haul up sails was good training as well.

In the 1920s, tug-of-war became a serious organized sport. Today the sport has a comprehensive set of rules and customs. National and world championships are held at different weight totals.

There are eight men in a tug-of-war team. According to the combined weight of the contestants the team will compete in one of a number of categories. Usually the lightest total is 560 kilograms.

There are three signals. At the first the teams pick up the rope. At the second they take the strain. At the third they pull. The rope is usually between 10 and 12 centimetres in circumference. When they are told to heave, the teams try and pull one another over a line which is marked on the ground.

Heave! Months of training are over and the team is in action. Tug-of-war teams try to train together at least twice a week before competitions, so that they are ready for anything.

The name given to the athlete stationed at the end of the rope is 'the anchor man' (inset). He drapes the rope over one shoulder and under his arm. He is often the heaviest competitor.

Archery
History of Archery

The invention of the bow about 8,000 years ago made a great difference to the lives of men and women. It meant that for the first time they could kill from a considerable distance, much farther than a spear could be thrown.

At first people used bows and arrows to hunt animals and birds, but then they began to see how they could be used as weapons of war. The Egyptians first used them on a large scale in their war against the Persians. Their arrows out-distanced the sling-shots and javelins of their enemies. The Persians were defeated and the Egyptians became a great power.

Etruscan warriors (above), armed with bows and arrows, conquered northern Italy 3,000 years ago.

The first men and women to use bows and arrows came from the south and east of Europe. We know something of the way of life of these Neolithic people because they painted scenes like this one (right) on the walls of caves.

This 11th-century archer is hunting. Archery was considered to be a pursuit of the lower orders, not the aristocracy.

For hundreds of years the bow remained the world's major weapon of destruction. The Romans used both the long-bow and the cross-bow. Invading Vikings cut down their foes with a hail of arrows. Turkish archers on small horses slew the Crusaders in the Middle East. When Ghengis Khan set out to conquer the world, he took with him bowmen on horseback. The bows they used were two metres long and the arrows less than a metre in length.

The English adopted the bow as a weapon from the Norsemen. In the Middle Ages, English long-bowmen were judged to be the best in Europe. Their bows were made of yew, elm or ash. The arrows were tipped with cowhorn. The strings of the bows were made of silk or hemp.

Archers carried 24 arrows in a belt. When they were not using them, they removed the strings from their bows in order to preserve them.

Egyptians hunted with the bow about 1400 BC. When the young Egyptian king Tutankhamun (above) died, 27 of his bows were buried with him, a sign of the regard in which the Egyptians held the skill.

By the 14th century, English kings had decided to adopt the bow as the principal weapon of their armies, instead of the lance, which had been used most before. In order to make sure that his subjects practised with the bow, Edward III banned them from playing football and ordered that 'everyone strong in body, at leisure on holidays, should use in their recreation bows and arrows'. Edward IV instructed all Englishmen to make sure that their children were taught how to use the bow.

Local authorities saw to it that butts, complete with targets, were set up so that citizens could practise their archery on Sundays.

In the 16th century, the increased use of gunpowder led to the long-bow being considered a less effective weapon in war. By this time, however, archery had become popular as a national sport in England and elsewhere.

When the first explorers moved into the interior of North America, they found that the Red Indians were skilful with the bow. As well as using it as a weapon of war and for hunting, the Red Indian tribes held their own competitions to choose the best shots.

The ancient Persians had many legends about a great huntsman called Kessi, who was famed for his ability with the bow. One day, in search of food, Kessi passed the dragon guarding the sun god's house (above). The god turned him into a star, the constellation Orion.

The supremacy of the English bowmen was proved in three decisive battles against the French in the 14th and 15th centuries. The French bow-men were equipped with cross-bows, but still the English triumphed (left). They fired their arrows from a distance of about 100 metres, and an onlooker at one of the battles said that the arrows fell as thick as snow upon the French.

The Samurai (right) were the professional warriors of old Japan. They swore allegiance to a master and fought to the death for him. Their code of conduct was called the 'bushido' or 'way of the warrior'. All Samurai were experts with different weapons, especially the sword and bow.

The Longbow

In the Middle Ages the men of Cheshire and Cornwall were said to be particularly skilled with the long bow. Today the sport is universal. There are two main types of bow in use – the straight, based on the traditional English model, and the recurved, which is a variation on the sort of bow once used in the Middle East.

Those bows which are made out of a single piece of material are known as 'self' bows, while the ones fashioned from several pieces joined together are known as 'backed' bows. Modern bows are made of yew and hickory wood, and from tubular steel or fibre-glass. Linen or Dacron are used for the strings, while wood, aluminium tubing or fibre-glass are used for the arrows.

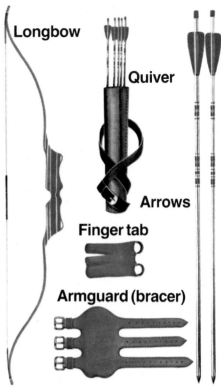

Longbow

Quiver

Arrows

Finger tab

Armguard (bracer)

To practise his sport the archer needs a bow, a number of arrows and a quiver in which to keep them. The quiver may be strapped to the archer's back or allowed to dangle from a belt. An armguard is worn on the wrist of the hand holding the bow. On the other hand a glove or leather tab will protect the fingers which draw back the bow-string.

Most novice archers will begin by taking part in 'target-shooting'. For this a circular straw target is used. This is divided into a number of col-oured 'zones', and the centre of the target is known as the Gold.

Archers who show ability go on to 'field archery' (left). Fourteen targets of varying sizes are placed round a course. The archer proceeds from target to target, firing at them from different distances.

Another form of archery is 'flight shooting'. In this the archers use arrows and very powerful bows.

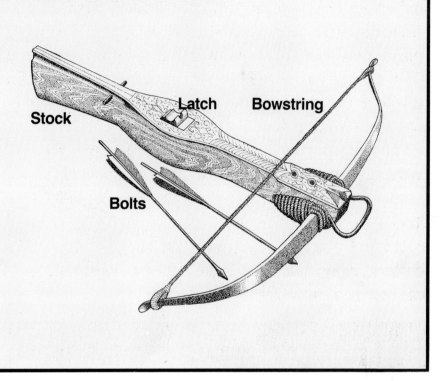

THE CROSSBOW IN HISTORY

The story of the Swiss national hero, William Tell, and the apple is a popular legend which has contributed greatly to the historical fame of the cross bow as a weapon of war. When Tell was taken prisoner by the local landowner, he was promised his liberty if he could shoot an apple in two which was placed on his son's head. He succeeded in doing this, but confessed that, if he had hit his son, the other arrow in his hand was intended for Gessler, the Austrian governor. He was arrested again, but managed to escape. He later killed Gessler, and became a legend in his own lifetime.

Stock   **Latch**   **Bowstring**   **Bolts**

The Crossbow

The cross bow was once considered more effective than the long bow, but it took too long to re-load it in battle. This weapon consisted of a very powerful bow fixed to a heavy bar. It fired short arrows called 'bolts'. The first cross bows were made of wood and horn, but later models were fashioned out of steel.

Considerable strength was needed to load the cross bow. Earlier versions had a stirrup attached, so that an archer could put his foot through it on the ground in order to steady himself. Later models were loaded by winding back a handle.

In 1139, the Church thought the cross bow was such a dreadful weapon that it tried to have it banned as a weapon of war. After the wars between England and France in the 14th and 15th centuries, however, the cross bow was superseded by the long bow. In the Second World War, crossbows were used again on commando raids by troops wishing to kill enemy sentries silently.

The bow of a cross bow is fixed horizontally across the end of a stock. An arrow is placed in the groove carved in the stock. The archer draws back the bow-string and secures in behind the catch, and the weapon is fired by squeezing a trigger.

How to Shoot with a Longbow

1

2

3

There are four stages in firing an arrow:

1. Fixing the string to the bow. One loop is placed over the end of the bow and slid down to the middle of the bow. The second loop is then fixed into position at the other end of the bow. The bow is braced under the arch of the foot while the first loop is slipped back up into position.

2. Nocking. This is the name given to putting the arrow into place. The bow is held horizontally and the arrow is fixed on the string.

3. Drawing. The bow-string is held with the first three fingers, with the arrow held between the first and second fingers. The bow arm is directed at the target. The elbow of the arm drawing back the string should be at shoulder level. When the string is brushing the archer's nose and chin it is in position.

4. Checking the score. Scoring methods vary, but the usual scores for the different colour zones are Gold 9, Red 7, Blue 5, Black 3 and White 1.

Archery is an international sport in which hundreds of thousands of men and women are involved all over the world. There are different types of competition open to all experienced bowmen and bow-women.

In most competitions a number of 'ends' are shot. An end consists of six arrows being fired. A competition is called a 'round'. There are various kinds of rounds, such as the York and the Hereford. In these two rounds, for example, 25 ends are shot.

Each round has its stated distances from which the arrows must be fired at the target. Competitors start at the distance the farthest from the target, fire their arrows and then advance to the next mark from which they are to fire at the target.

There are national and international governing bodies for the sport. These hold their championships for the best archers from each region. There are also tournaments in which children can take part, shooting with special bows.

Competitive Archery

The universal popularity of the bow is shown by the number of stories connected with it, some of them true and some of them folk-legend.

One English king, William Rufus, was killed by an arrow while hunting in the New Forest. One of his companions fired at a stag. The arrow missed its mark and struck the king.

Perhaps the most popular hero to be associated with the bow is Robin Hood. It is difficult to find out how much of this outlaw's story is true, but legend has it that he and his band of 'merry men' lived in Sherwood Forest and stole from the rich to give to the poor.

Many Red Indians, including Hiawatha, were also said to be great exponents with the bow.

Archery involves the use of the muscles of the upper body and is a sport in which disabled people may take part (above). There are separate tournaments for the disabled, but many men and women take part in ordinary tournaments from their wheelchairs.

Women competitors can be seen (right) in the 1972 Olympics held in Munich.

Competitors line up at a tournament (left). After an 'end' of six arrows the competitors will approach the targets to check their scores.

Bowmen throughout history have been reputed to have performed marvels with the bow. It is easier, however, to check on the records of modern performers. A number of them have sent arrows a great distance. In 1970, Harry Drake of the USA sent an arrow well over 1,000 metres with a cross-bow. One of the greatest of all women archers, Mrs. M. Howell, won the American championship 17 times between 1883 and 1907. A favourite trick performed by some professionals is to fire an arrow into the Gold, and then split the first arrow with a second!

The Javelin

The spear was one of the first weapons invented by men. In its original form it was just a pointed stick, but this was later improved upon, and it became a wooden shaft with a flint point fixed to the end. At first it was a weapon which was used to jab and prod, but it became more useful when it was thrown. The major drawback to this was that once the weapon had been thrown it left the warrior defenceless.

The basic aim of the javelin thrower is to hurl his javelin from behind a line and see how far he can make it travel through the air. The run up before the throw is very important, as may be seen in this picture of Fatima Whitbread about to throw (right). A mark is placed on the ground to let the athlete know that the throwing-line is near, so that she does not step over it.

Most of the early civilizations used the spear as one of their major weapons of war. The Greeks carried very long spears and used them in the military formation known as the 'phalanx'. Holding their spears before them, a company of soldiers would try and drive their opponents back as the Greeks slowly advanced.

The Greeks introduced spear-throwing into their athletic competitions, particularly in the Olympic Games. A thong fixed to the shaft helped the athlete gain distance.

A famous Russian javelin thrower, Makarov, is about to release the javelin (above). The metal point of the javelin must strike the ground first for the throw to be recognized, but it does not have to stick in the ground. Both men and women may compete in javelin competitions but the javelins are of different sizes. There is no limit to the length of approach.

Boxing
Early Boxing

Primitive men probably used a mixture of fighting and wrestling when they met their enemies, but organized fist fighting did not become really popular until the time of a Greek monarch called Thesus, about 900 BC.

The bloodthirsty Thesus made his gladiators sit on stone slabs facing each other with their fists wrapped in leather thongs. The gladiators would punch away at one another until one of them was dead.

The Roman seen resting (right) would have had to be prepared to fight to the death in the arena. The best-known of all the gladiator-boxers was Damoxene of Syracuse. He was so terrible in his punching power that he was banned from all tournaments after a contest with another professional boxer, a man called Kreugas.

Boxing in Greek times was often included in the vicious all-in combat known as the 'pankration', but individual bouts were also held (below).

The dreaded cestus, a primitive form of boxing glove, was made of leather, wood or stone and was bound to the hand with thongs. The development of the cestus meant that it was possible for a boxer to kill his opponent. Crowds flocked to the arena to see gladiators batter one another to death.

Bareknuckle Boxing

After the end of the Roman empire, boxing was neglected as a sport for hundreds of years. It surfaced again in England in the 17th century, when men took to settling their differences with their fists. Some of these 'grudge fights' attracted large crowds, and people began paying for the privilege of watching.

At first contests took place indoors upon a raised stage, but the halls could not contain all the people who wanted to watch. The bouts were transferred to the open air, with rings pitched upon moors and plains.

These early fights took place between pugilists fighting with bare fists. A round ended when a man was knocked down. He had 30 seconds in which to recover and return to the mark in the centre of the ring.

The sport became popular with the nobility as well as with the masses. The Duke of Cumberland, the son of George II, took an interest in prize-fighting.

John Gully (above) became champion on the retirement of Hen Pearce.

James Figg (left), the first prize-fighting champion of England, claimed the title in 1719 and retired undefeated in 1730. Jack Broughton (far left), Figg's pupil, became the bare-knuckle champion, and in 1743 drew up the first set of rules for the sport.

In the 18th century, criminals and gamblers took over the prize ring. Contests were 'fixed', the results being arranged in advance.

The sport regained its popularity when international matches between American and British fighters attracted large crowds. Prize-fighting was made illegal, but the contests were still held.

The first great American prize-fighter was a black man called Bill Richmond. After knocking out three British soldiers in a tavern brawl he turned professional, backed by the Duke of Northumberland. Richmond won many fights in Britain, the last when he was 56 years old.

One bare-knuckle contest in Melbourne, Australia in 1856, between James Kelly and Jack Smith, lasted for six hours and fifteen minutes. Skin-tight gloves to protect the hands were introduced, but this did not make the bouts any shorter. In New Orleans in 1893, Andy Bowen and Jack Burke, 'the Irish Lad', boxed a draw over 110 rounds, taking seven hours and ten minutes.

The first visitors to the 'friendly islands' of Tonga found that women were keen fighters (above).

One of the last great bare-knuckle contests (below) took place in France in 1888 between John L. Sullivan, American world champion, and the British champion, Charlie Mitchell.

Glovefighters

Changes took place at the end of the 19th century when the Queensberry rules were generally adopted. No bout could go longer than 20 rounds, and each round lasted three minutes. Gloves had to weigh at least 170 grams. If a boxer was knocked down he had ten seconds in which to regain his feet. A contest which lasted the full distance was decided on the points scored.

Boxers were also divided into weight divisions, from flyweight (under 50.802 kgs) to heavyweight (over 79.378 kgs). Championships were introduced at all weights.

It was generally agreed that there were only six basic blows in boxing – the straight left and straight right, the left hook and right hook, and the left upper-cut and right upper-cut.

Jack Johnson was the first black man to win the heavyweight championship of the world, but he was very unpopular with boxing fans. In Reno in 1910 he fought a former heavyweight champion, James J. Jeffries (right), before a huge crowd. Jeffries was defeated in 15 rounds.

One of the most thrilling of all heavyweight contests was in 1923, when Jack Dempsey knocked out Luis Firpo, the South American champion in the second round. Dempsey had knocked Firpo down seven times in the first round, but Firpo knocked the world champion right out of the ring (below).

Every country seemed to produce great boxers. From Australia there was Young Griffo, so skilful that he could stand on a handkerchief, hands at his sides, and avoid punches thrown merely by moving his head.

Wales had Jimmy Wilde, weighing less than 50 kgs but called 'the ghost with a hammer in his hand' because he could knock out opponents weighing up to 58 kgs.

Most boxers showed great courage, but one of the bravest was the Frenchman, Eugène Criqui. His jaw was shattered in the First World War and replaced with the jawbone of a sheep, but Criqui still went on to win the featherweight championship of the world.

In 1959 the Swede, Ingemar Johansson, surprised everyone by knocking out Floyd Patterson for the world title.

The black fighter, Joe Louis, held the world title for 12 years and defended it successfully 25 times. Here, he is defending his championship (left) against Arturo Godoy.

In 1973 in Jamaica, Joe Frazier defended his world title against George Foreman (below). Frazier was surprisingly knocked out by Foreman in two rounds.

55

Title Fights

Successful boxers have always made a great deal of money from the ring. As early as 1805, Hen Pearce received £1,000 for fighting John Gully, an enormous sum for those days. More than a century later, in 1927, Gene Tunney was paid almost a million dollars for defending his title against Jack Dempsey.

The biggest money-earner of all time, however, is Muhammad Ali, who won the heavyweight championship in 1965. Fighting before enormous audiences on television, Ali has received as much as five million dollars for a single contest.

Most young men who wish to become professional boxers have first of all to gain experience by fighting as amateurs. Amateur contests last only three rounds and are very carefully supervised. Starting as a novice, a youngster can go on to enter the national amateur championships. If he does well in these he may attract the attention of a manager and be invited to box for money as a professional.

The young professional will be carefully matched against other men of limited experience, and will fight only six- and eight-round bouts. If he does well in these he may progress to the more demanding ten- and twelve-round contests.

The young professional will almost certainly have to keep on his day-time job, and do his training in the evening and at weekends. This is a very demanding routine, and many aspiring professionals find out that boxing is not for them at this stage.

Eventually, a matchmaker working for a big boxing promoter may decide that the boxer is ready to fight for a championship. Contracts will be signed and the young fighter will go into serious training. If the boxer manages to win a regional or national championship he can then begin to think of the world title.

Muhammad Ali, 'I am the greatest!' is seen (right) in his championship contest with Cleveland Williams in 1966.

A former Olympic light-heavyweight champion, Ali has earned more money as a professional than any other boxer.

The Fight

All boxers, whether professional or amateur, have to train hard in the gymnasium (left) for their contests. Well muffled up, they engage in shadow-boxing, skipping and a variety of floor exercises. With the exception of the heavyweights, all boxers have to watch their weight carefully to make sure that they remain in their correct weight division.

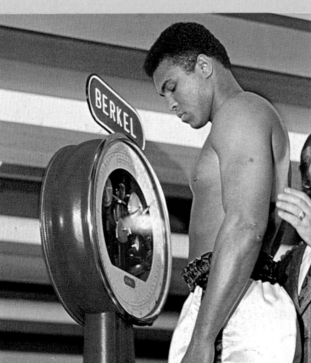

Muhammad Ali is seen on the scales (left). For most bouts, the weigh-in takes place at noon on the day of a contest. At the same time the boxers undergo a medical examination. Heavyweights are allowed to come in at any weight, but all other boxers agree in their contract to appear under a certain weight. If they weigh more, they are given a short time to lose weight, or else they have to pay a fine.

George Foreman at work on the heavy bag (right). A boxer punches away at a bag of this sort in order to build up his strength and improve his punching power. Another type of punch-ball, with the ball descending from a platform, is used to develop a boxer's speed of punch. Special gloves are used for punch-bag work to protect the fighter's hands.

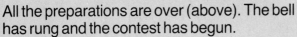

All the preparations are over (above). The bell has rung and the contest has begun.

A boxer's hands are his main assets. They are protected in a contest by having metres of tape wound round them (right) before the gloves are put on. When the tape is wound on, a representative of the opposing boxer is always present.

Some Heavyweight Champions

John L. Sullivan was born in the USA in 1858. Nicknamed 'the Boston Strong Boy', he was the last of the bare-knuckle champions. He won the title by knocking out Paddy Ryan in nine rounds at Mississippi City in 1882. A bluff, hearty character, Sullivan capitalized on his fame by touring the USA, offering a thousand dollars to any man who could last four rounds.

Bob Fitzsimmons was born in England in 1862, but spent most of his youth in New Zealand. He knocked out James J. Corbett for the title in Carson City, Nevada in 1897. Fitzsimmons was incredibly light for a heavyweight, weighing only 75 kgs. He was renowned for his famous 'solar-plexus' punch.

Jack Johnson, the first coloured heavyweight champion, was born in Galveston, Texas in 1878. A superb defensive boxer with a hard punch, Johnson took the championship from the Canadian Tommy Burns after James J. Jeffries retired undefeated. Johnson was an unpopular champion and was defeated in 1915 by Jess Willard, who knocked him out in 26 rounds.

Jess Willard was born in Kansas in 1881. He was the tallest of all the champions, but was a gentle, docile man who did not take up boxing until he was 28 years old. He developed a reputation as a fearsome puncher after he had killed one opponent, Bull Young, with a single punch.

Jack Dempsey, 'the Manassa Mauler' became of the most famous of all the fighters. Before winning the title, he spent years as a hobo, wandering from town to town, fighting in saloons just for the price of a meal. Afterwards, Dempsey defended his title on a number of occasions. He was outpointed for the championship by Gene Tunney in 1926.

Primo Carnera was the first Italian to win the world championship, knocking out Jack Sharkey in six rounds in 1933. Carnera was the biggest champion of his time and was nicknamed 'the Ambling Alp'. Once a circus strongman he had been persuaded into becoming a professional boxer, but he was not an outstanding champion.

Joe Louis was born in Alabama in 1914. Known as 'the Brown Bomber', he knocked out James J. Braddock for the title in eight rounds in 1937. Louis was the grandson of a slave, and he was brought up in a cabin with 12 other children before going to work in an automobile factory. He defeated a number of former champions, including Primo Carnera and Max Baer.

Rocky Marciano was the first white man to win the title for 15 years. A small man for a heavyweight, Marciano made up for his short reach by non-stop attack. He swarmed all over his opponents, wearing them down. In 1952, he knocked out Joe Louis. Marciano defended his title six times and retired undefeated.

Floyd Patterson won an Olympic boxing gold medal at the age of 17. He became world professional champion at the age of 21, after Marciano retired. He was an excellent boxer and a hard hitter, but lacked self-confidence. He was liable to walk into punches and get knocked down, but he usually got up again and won.

Sonny Liston was a powerfully built, ponderous fighter who was often in trouble with the law and spent some time in prison. He established an impressive record as a heavyweight boxer, losing only one of his first 30 contests. He claimed that the only reason for this defeat was that, while he was laughing at the antics of his opponent, his adversary suddenly came back and hit him, breaking his jaw!

Muhammad Ali was born in Louisville, Kentucky in 1942 and is considered one of boxing's greatest champions and one of the sport's best-known personalities. A superb boxer and very fast on his feet, he won the Olympic light-heavyweight gold medal in 1960 and then turned professional. Ali defended the title on a number of occasions, until he was outpointed in 1978 in Las Vegas by Leon Spinks.

Larry Holmes, 'the Black Cloud' from Easton in Pennsylvania, outpointed Ken Norton in 1978 for the vacant title. In 1979 John Tate also claimed the title, but Holmes was still considered by most people to be the holder, and in 1980 defeated Ali.

Boxing Variations

Different types of boxing have emerged all over the world and some are still practised today. The ancient Greeks had a vicious form of all-in fighting called the 'pankration', which involved boxing, wrestling and gouging, and the Chinese developed a similar style.

In France a form of boxing which allowed kicking was also popular, and the practitioners developed great skill in the use of their fists and feet. A version of this sport is still practised in Thailand.

In the rings of North America the 'battle royal' used to consist of six boxers who were put in the ring at the same time. The winner was the one who was still on his feet at the end of the contest.

Also in North America a type of fist-fighting used by the lumberjacks of Canada meant that two men were strapped in a seated position on a bench facing one another, and then encouraged to punch away at each other.

The grace and agility of Thai boxing is seen here as one boxer lands a kick high on the head of his opponent. Orthodox boxing is also popular in Thailand, and Chartchai Chionoi won the world flyweight championship in 1973.

Stickplay

The Oriental nations have perfected a number of fighting sports involving the simple wooden staff from the ancient forms of self-defence. Staves were originally used by the wandering monks of the Far East. In order to fend off bandits, as a form of self-defence, some of them developed the use of this stickplay into a high art.

Two of the most common forms of stickplay used today are 'bodo' and 'jodo'. In bodo, a long staff, about two metres in length, is used. Jodo favours the short, light stick. There are many techniques and routines to be learned in both styles. In both forms, neither masks or body armour are used.

'Naginata-do' is practised almost exclusively by women and girls. It is executed with a staff some three metres in length. This is held in both hands and used with long, sweeping movements. Armour and masks are used.

The wooden sword known as the 'bokken' is used in a number of fighting sports like karate, and also by itself. In some mock combats the wooden spear, the 'yari', is used to sweep the legs of an opponent from beneath him. The moves are often centuries old.

Perhaps the most unusual wooden weapons used in the fighting sports of today originated on the island of Okinawa hundreds of years ago. The invading Japanese forbade the islanders to carry or use weapons. As a result of this, many Okinawans taught themselves to fight with wooden tools and implements like the sickle and the rice-husker. Such implements are still used in fighting sports on the island, but are now used elsewhere as well.

The most popular form of stickplay is 'kendo', sword-fighting in which wooden swords are used. Millions of people all over the world take part in this sport.

Great agility and speed are needed in all forms of stick-play. The moves have to be carried out at high speed.

In this exhibition of wu shu, the competitor with the spear is attacking, while his opponent ducks the blow.

The Samurai

The professional warriors known as the Samurai were well established in Japan by the 13th century. They achieved great skill in all types of warfare and with a wide range of weapons.

They lived and died by a strict set of rules. Some of these regulations were later carried over into the fighting sports which emerged from the practices of the Samurai. These warriors believed that everything had to be done in an arranged and honourable way. In battle, for example, there must be no fear of death.

The Samurai paid a great deal of attention to their equipment. There were 23 items of armour that a warrior had to wear, in addition to a battery of weapons. There was even a special bag in which to place the severed head of a vanquished foe. In the siege of Osaka in 1615, the Samurai even used firearms.

A Samurai swordsman was supposed to be able to cleave an opponent in half with one stroke of his sword (above).

The Samurai took part on both sides in the siege of Osaka in 1614 (below).

When they were not actually fighting for a master, the Japanese warriors were constantly training in the use of the sword, the bow and other weapons. They also practised the arts of modesty, humility, gentleness and chivalry at the tea-ceremonies that they attended between battles. These very formal ceremonies were part of a ritual which the warriors considered essential to their victories.

The horse was an important possession of the Samurai. The warrior would often ride into battle loudly declaiming his name and those of his important ancestors, and insisting that an opponent of equal status be sent forth to meet him in single combat.

In 1867 power passed to the Emperor of Japan, who had no need of the warriors. The war arts were turned into the fighting sports of today (above).

The Samurai trained hard, but by the end of the 19th century their great days were coming to an end. These two (right) seem aware of that fact.

The Samurai first came to prominence in a great war in Japan from 1180 until 1185, known as the Gempei War. Professional warriors fought with great distinction on both sides. By the end of the war, the Samurai were well established as warriors. For centuries they roamed the country, sometimes in small bands, sometimes in armies.

In 1274 and 1281, Samurai armies beat off invasions by the Mongols. Throughout the turbulent 15th and 16th centuries, groups of Samurai fought for various causes all over Japan. By 1592, they were gathering together again to invade Korea before going on to attack China.

There were said to be half a million Samurai warriors in Japan at the movement's peak in the 17th century, each man trained and dedicated to his cause. Those who could find no master to serve worked as trainers and teachers.

Unarmed Combat

One of the fastest-growing forms of unarmed combat in the 1970s and 1980s was karate, which means 'Chinese hands'. The sport dates back hundreds of years. Although it originated in China, karate was perfected on the island of Okinawa as a means of resistance to the occupying Japanese. It can be practised by both men and women.

Judo (Ju-jitsu)

There are a number of different explanations of the origins of the fighting sport of judo.

There is one story that the idea came from a Japanese doctor. In the middle of a snow-storm, when the branches of many trees were cracking beneath the weight of piled-up snow, one tree remained upright. This was the slim willow whose branches were so pliable that the snow slipped constantly from them. Observing this, the doctor, it is said, devised a form of self-defence in which flexibility and suppleness were all-important. This was ju-jitsu, later to become judo.

Another story is that the sport was introduced into Japan by Chinese Buddhist monks, who developed a form of unarmed combat as a means of self-defence on their wanderings. They could in this way ward off attacks by bandits. The Japanese then turned the art into an attacking sport as well as a defensive one.

The art of judo consists of a series of holds, throws and falls in which a man or woman, or even a child, tries to use an opponent's strength against him (above).

Gradually, high-ranking judo exponents were allowed to leave Japan and teach their art overseas. As early as 1905, the French police were receiving instruction in the art (left). The police forces of several large cities in the USA followed suit. Before long there were judo schools all over the world. Today, judo is an extremely popular fighting sport.

Samurai warriors took up ju-jitsu so that they could continue to fight if they were disarmed during a battle.

The modern form of judo was adapted from ju-jitsu by the Japanese professor Jigoro Kano, who opened his first school in 1882, with nine pupils.

Kano developed judo into a fine and subtle art. A system of coloured belts leading up to the sought-after black belt was later devised. Students had to learn the vulnerable parts of the human body. During a four-year course they had to go on a diet of rice, fruit and fish. The sport could be adopted by the young and by women. This meant that experts could defend themselves against much larger opponents and even against a number of adversaries attacking at the same time. Judo is now a very popular form of self-defence.

Wearing the uniform of long, loose-fitting jacket and trousers, the judo practitioner is upgraded from belt to belt. The belts in ascending order of importance are white, yellow, orange, green, blue, brown and black. There are a number of degrees of 'dans' to the black belt and to rise in these takes enormous dedication and skill. The first thing to learn is how to fall correctly. Once this has been mastered, a man or a woman can go on to learn the many throws, holds and locks involved.

Kung Fu

Kung fu is the general name given to all the fighting arts of China. There are many of these forms of combat, most of them dating back thousands of years. In China and Hong Kong these fighting arts are still separate and distinct. In the western world, however, aspects of the different fighting sports of China are usually mixed to form the one known as kung fu.

The sport became very popular in the USA in the 1970s. This was because of the success of a weekly television drama series called simply 'Kung Fu'. Set in the days of the Chinese emperors, it followed the exploits of a Chinese American skilled in the Chinese fighting arts. The series showed the hero, played by the actor David Carradine, learning the arts of kung fu, taking them to North America and then using them in a series of adventures.

In the People's Republic of China, the martial arts are still practised, but here they are more generally known as 'wu shu', instead of kung fu, the term used in Hong Kong and the West.

Although many different styles are used in kung fu, great importance is placed on speed and agility. The true kung fu artist is very athletic and can move as lightly and gracefully as a ballet dancer.

Most forms of kung fu are extremely graceful. One type, known as the dragon style, consists of the practitioners moving in a zig-zag fashion like the dragon of legends. Experts at the dragon style advance and retreat rapidly.

A spectacular aspect of kung fu consists of breaking bricks and lumps of wood with the head (left) or the edge of the hand. For this a person practises for many years. He needs to acquire a tough head and tough hands to do it in safety.

One of the best known component parts of kung fu fighting is the acrobatic use of kicking. This is called Shaolin, after the temple in North China where it originated. The Shaolin artist always faces his opponent in a sideways posture, almost like a crab, in order to present as small a target as possible. He will then launch himself into a series of dazzling kicks from all angles, spinning in the air like a top. He will kick with different parts of the foot – the ball, the side, the heel and the toe.

The term 'kung fu' means 'human effort', and the practice of this sport emphasizes the meaning of the words. Its exponents must be very fit and agile, as speed of movement is essential in overcoming an opponent.

Another effective fighting sport used in kung fu is the one known as Chin Na. This means 'capture and hold'. Hundreds of years ago it was taught to Chinese officials so that they could subdue wrong-doers and bring them to justice without harming them unduly in the process. A series of numbing blows and holds will overcome the most aggressive adversary.

A man who did much to make fighting sports popular in the USA was the film-star Bruce Lee, seen here (above) in action. Brought up in Hong Kong he became adept in kung fu, karate and aiki-do. His good looks and strong personality took him into films.

Aiki-do

Aiki-do was devised by a Japanese master of unarmed combat, Ueshiba Morihei. A weak and sickly child, he built up his strength and physique by sheer determination. At the age of 20 he set off in search of a way of life which would combine his regard for health and fitness with full use of the mind and will-power.

As a result of his dedication, Morihei slowly devised aiki-do. He did not believe in violence, thinking that it should only be used as a last resort.

When he was ready, he opened a school for his new art in Tokyo, teaching that it was essential to achieve harmony of body and spirit, that both must come together before a man can accomplish anything worthwhile.

Great masters of all forms of unarmed combat flocked to Ueshiba Morihei's school. The art flourished for most of the 20th century. After the Second World War, however, when Japan was occupied by the victorious Americans, all forms of unarmed combat were banned and did not emerge again for some years. When the martial arts were once again allowed, aiki-do regained its place.

Today aiki-do is practised in many countries (right). Great importance is placed on concentration, relaxation and correct breathing. It was once rumoured that an aiki-do star could overcome an opponent merely by thinking about him! Some throws are spectacular.

Karate

Karate is an international fighting sport in which a fast-moving man or woman attempts to strike at certain target areas of an opponent's body, using fists, feet, knees, fingers and the edge of the hand.

The sport was introduced to the island of Okinawa from the mainland of China. At the beginning of the 20th century it was exported to Japan. A number of different schools of karate came into operation there, until in the end more than 50 separate styles were being taught by masters of the fighting art.

After the Second World War, many American service-men stationed in the Far East became fascinated by karate with its spectacular kicks and blows. The breaking of piles of bricks with the edge of the hand also helped to make karate an intriguing sport.

By the 1950s there were a number of karate schools in North America. Ten years later there were professional championships open to all-comers. Karate was also taken up by television and film-stars wishing to display impressive ways of overcoming their foes on the screen.

A punch in karate usually travels in a straight line while striking blows are delivered with a chopping motion. Both methods have to be learned at karate schools (above).

Pupils at a karate school have much to learn. Before they master the different attacking techniques, they must perfect a defensive system which is known as blocking (right).

Karate Blows and Moves

Many karate blows are delivered with the edge of the open hand, using a chopping motion. The arm is snapped out from the elbow with great speed before returning to its original position.

Considerable practice in the various karate kicks is essential. Balance has to be maintained while the knee of the kicking foot is raised high to gain force and impetus.

Sparring with an opponent is a vital part of the training of a karate student. This helps to develop timing. Many of the techniques of sparring are almost like formal dances.

High kicks are dramatic and thrilling to watch in karate demonstrations, but they are used with caution by experts as they tend to leave the kicker in an unbalanced position.

Advanced exponents of karate can shatter a plank with a bare-footed kick, leaping high into the air. The most powerful kicks are often delivered with the heel.

Throwing techniques are not as important in karate as in some forms of unarmed combat. The masters of the art, however, include a number of throws in their repertoires.

In some advanced forms of karate practised by leading exponents in Japan, fighters allow kicks and blows to penetrate their guards in order to toughen them up.

Among the many modern schools of karate in Japan there is one which teaches the art to Buddhist monks as part of their training. The Oriental schools consider meditation and concentration an important part of the preparation of any exponent of the art of karate. Opponents must be treated with great honour and consideration. Masters try to encourage their pupils to study karate for the physical, spiritual and mental benefits it will bring, and not for the sake of winning bouts.

Tai-chi-chuan

Tai-chi-chuan is the ancient art of Chinese boxing, sometimes known as shadow-boxing.

The art was developed in the Taoist temples by monks. A legend has it that the originator of the fighting sport once saw a snake overcome an attacking hawk with sinuous and graceful movements, striking it suddenly with deadly accuracy.

Accordingly, tai-chi-chuan was developed as a means of exercise and discipline among the monks. The phrase means 'great final fist'. The training and exercise involved in tai-chi-chuan meant that its practitioners could, in the last resort, defend themselves against all attackers, especially bandits.

One of the underlying principles of the art was that every man has one weak point. The tai-chi-chuan expert was trained to seek out this weak point and concentrate on it when fighting an opponent. The monks practised the art early in the morning, and today its followers are urged to train soon after dawn.

Tai-chi-chuan is practised on its own, and is also included in the two martial arts known as wu shu (above and right) in China and kung fu in the West.

Flying leaps are involved in the fighting sport as well as prods and punches. The movements involved are said to exercise the muscles of the body.

Throwing Sports

Throwing weapons were developed by primitive people in an effort to place as much distance as possible between the thrower and his prey or enemy.

In different parts of the world men and women tried various throwing implements in order to find out which was the most useful and effective.

Some tried hurling flat, circular stones through the air at adversaries or skimming them across the surface of lakes at water-creatures. Other used curved sticks, curling them through the air to hit targets from unusual angles. Most, however, were contented with straight, pointed sticks which could be hurled at the enemy.

From these early throwing experiments developed some of the basic weapons of war among the first peoples, which in time were adopted for some modern fighting sports. Some of the first warriors to use spears and javelins on a large scale were the Sumerians, who lived on a plain near the River Tigris.

The boomerang, like this one (above) from Western Australia, is one of the oldest weapons known to man and is still used by the Australian aborigines. There are different types of boomerang. Those used in war are not designed to return to the men throwing them. The hunting boomerangs used today are thrown with a wrist action which spins them through the air in such a fashion that, after striking a target a glancing blow, they return to the throwers. In modern sports the boomerang displays the skill of the thrower.

Darts has long been a popular sport in pubs and clubs, but for a long time it was thought to be of limited interest. In the 1970s, however, it became popular on television (left) and has gained a vast new audience.

Smaller pointed weapons were used in Africa and Malaysia, where darts were placed in blow-pipes and aimed at foes. Flat circular stones proved too cumbersome to use in battle for long, but the Sikhs from India developed a flat steel ring called the 'chakram' which they threw at their enemies. Curved sticks were used in a number of parts of the world, but mainly in Australia where the use of the boomerang was perfected.

Among other throwing weapons were the South American 'bolas', ropes weighted at the end, and the Roman catapult, which launched huge stones through the air.

Both men and women can take part in the modern discus event. Women use a lighter discus than men, but athletes of both sexes have thrown more than 70 metres. The modern thrower stands in a circle 2.5 metres in diameter, holding the discus in the flat of the hand. The arm is swung backwards and forwards and then the discus is released with great speed. The event was included in the first Olympics.

Shooting

History of Shooting

Thousands of years ago the Chinese were using gunpowder for flares, but it was not until the friar, Bernard Schwartz, experimented with its explosive qualities in 14th-century Germany, that firearms were invented.

The first squat, unreliable cannons had to be trundled into position on waggons. The cannons consisted of metal barrels stuffed with gunpowder surrounding a stone ball. The gunpowder was lit through a hole in the barrel, the force of the explosion projecting the stone ball.

The first hand-guns were also big and clumsy, usually needing two men to fire them. In these a match was set to the gunpowder in the barrel, as it was with the cannon.

These early muskets were slowly developed. In the 17th century the old 'wheel-lock' type was superseded by the flintlock. Several hundreds of years later, metal cartridges were developed. In addition small hand-guns were also introduced and became popular.

A Portuguese soldier with his firearm (above). Loading and firing such weapons took a considerable time, so soldiers often protected the riflemen.

Buffalo Bill (right) was supposedly the greatest Indian scout of all time.

COLT AND THE PEACEMAKER

In 1836, the American Samuel Colt obtained his first patent for a six-barrelled rotating breech revolver, and founded a company to manufacture these weapons. This gun (below) is the 1873 version of the Colt 45, 'the gun that won the West'. Sometimes known as the 'Peacemaker', most of the US marshalls wore and used this hand-gun to good effect.

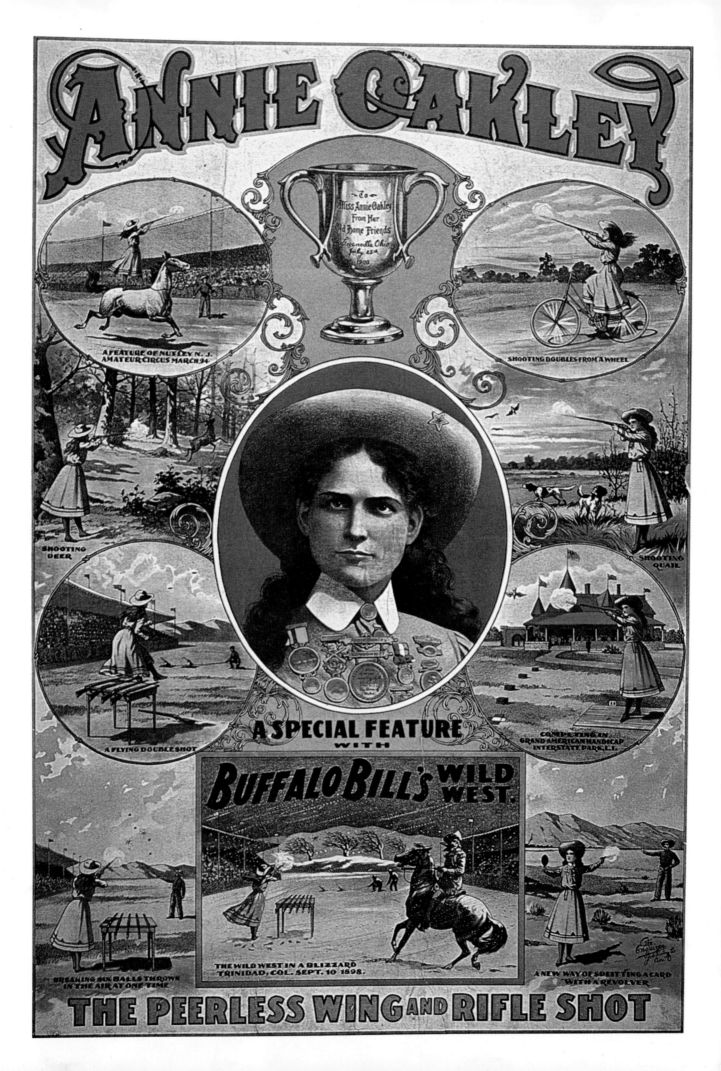

Members of the Metropolitan police force practising for a revolver-shooting competition (above).

One of the greatest women sharp-shooters of all time was Annie Oakley, 'Little Miss Sure-Shot' (left). After winning many local competitions, Annie was invited to join Buffalo Bill Cody's famous travelling circus. She was sometimes the victim of jealousy from the male sharp-shooters in the show. Her own firing was above reproach, but it was suggested that Buffalo Bill himself was not above loading his weapons with scatter-shot instead of single cartridges. This meant that he had a much greater chance of hitting the glass balls at which he was aiming.

History of Competitive Shooting

A number of bloody wars in the 19th century gave impetus to the sport of competitive rifle-shooting, and later of revolver shooting. In 1860, a firing range was set up on Wimbledon Common outside London. This received considerable publicity when Queen Victoria encouraged regular competitions, presenting a prize of £250.

A number of international shooting competitions took place between English and Irish teams. In 1871, an Irish team of sharp-shooters visited the USA. An American team defeated the Irish, giving the sport such popularity in the USA that, in 1872, 100,000 people watched the national championships.

When the British army fared badly against the Boers in the Boer War, there was a great demand from the British public for young men to be given instruction in the use of firearms, and this led to the formation of rifle clubs.

Modern Shooting

There have been many advances and improvements in the construction of firearms in the 20th century. Two world wars and many smaller conflicts have made the manufacture of arms a flourishing industry, so much so that the gun-makers are often referred to as the 'merchants of death'. For many years in Britain the Lee Enfield was the most popular rifle. Today it has many competitors in the form of light, strong steel rifles with magazines capable of holding up to 30 rounds of ammunition.

In recent years there have also been many alterations in the construction of pistols and revolvers. The requirements of hard-pressed law-enforcement agencies all over the world have led to the introduction of such heavy models as the Smith and Weston .44 Magnum. This is one of the heaviest and most explosive hand-guns ever devised.

Police forces and military organizations have also taken up sub-machine guns of various calibres, weapons which are capable of pouring out bullets and cartridges at a target. At the same time the interests of target-shooters have also been catered for with new types of pistols, revolvers and rifles appearing on the market. The demand for such weapons is considerable.

Shooting is one of the most popular of modern sports. This is regarded with great concern in some areas. In the USA, for example, where firearms are readily available in large quantities, many feel that there should be a rigorous form of licencing introduced.

Nevertheless, different aspects of the sport flourish. Target-shooting has many followers; hunting of deer and birds and other creatures is carried on all over the world; there are even societies in which men and women dress up as 19th-century cowboys and practise the fast-draw of the old gun-fighters.

Clay-pigeon shooting is popular with both men and women. Saucer-shaped objects are released from an automatic trap. They have to be shattered by the shooters as they fly upwards. The sport originated in the 1830s.

Competition shooting at targets with rifles from the prone position. Match shooting competitions and individual championships take place all over the world. Important venues in the history of the sport include Bisley in England and Camp Perry in the USA. Rules and regulations vary from country to country.

When firing from the standing position, the shooter usually stands at right angles to the target. The legs should be straight, with the body-weight well distributed. The shooter usually leans back a little and twists to the left. Resting the left arm against the rib cage, the rifle is supported in the left hand. The trigger is pulled with the trigger finger of the right hand.

A competitor is seen here lining up on the target through a sight. Telescopic sights are allowed in target-shooting, the sights being capable of adjustment. In Britain it is common that 1,000 metres are placed between the marksman and the target. Under international regulations, on the other hand, 300 metres is the distance favoured.

Great concentration is needed when a marksman is lining up a shot with a revolver, pistol or rifle. This man is wearing a pair of protective ear-muffs as the sound of the revolver firing could deafen him.

Jousting

Jousting at tournaments or mock battles was a popular pastime in Europe in the Middle Ages. Originally intended to provide knights with practice in all forms of combat, tournaments were also used as a means of toughening up young men and getting them used to hard knocks!

Jousts became a well-attended spectator sport and at some of the best-known tournaments hundreds of tents would be put up and the atmosphere was that of a combined holiday and fair.

One of the most favoured forms of mounted combat was that between two riders armed with lances. They would gallop full-tilt at one another and each would try to unseat the other. So many horses were badly hurt in these encounters that eventually a fence was put into position between the riders so that the mounts would not be injured. The techniques of jousting were also often used in the battlefield.

Some kings tried to ban tournaments. Not only were too many valuable knights getting hurt but violent enmities were developing between contestants, so that warriors in the same army often hated each other because of the result of a joust. In spite of this tournaments continued to flourish in many countries.

No great meeting or celebration was complete without a tournament. Heralds would be sent abroad to announce the time and place of forthcoming jousts, and knights flocked from all over to compete in the lists. Sometimes, on the last day of a tournament, all those who had taken part in it would be divided into two armies for one last great mock-battle. The knights often jousted with a favour from their lady tied to their arm. The winner of a joust was entitled to keep the horse and armour of his opponent. Today, jousts are still held at fairs around Britain.

The knights in this medieval scene have just ridden full-tilt at one another in a tournament.

Jousting often resulted in the death of one of the two opponents.

War Games

A most popular fighting sport of modern times is the War Game. In this, contestants dress in the costumes of days gone by and re-fight old battles, using blank ammunition and blunted swords. The Civil War Society re-enacts the wars between the Cavaliers and Roundheads in England.

The Roundhead pikemen advance in one picture and carry their flag in the other (above) while the Cavaliers fire their cannon (right), in a reconstruction of the Civil War.

Index